# DANCES OF DREAMS

For Robert —

# DANCES OF DREAMS

Poetry of Meditation (2012-2014)

by

Lama Karma Chötso

New York, New York

Published by MidTown Publishing Inc.
1001 Avenue of Americas
12th Floor
New York, NY 10018

Library of Congress Control Number:
2014940345

ISBN 978-1-62677-006-5
ISBN 978-1-62677-007-2 (e-book)


Printed in the United States of America
First Edition
1 3 5 7 9 10 8 6 4 2

# Praise of Dances of Dreams

Through language, two people connect to share and explore meaning that was previously unrevealed. All knowledge is grounded in imagery and symbol, and poetry in particular can convey truth through beauty. In the profound tradition of dharma poetry, exemplified by such works as the Hundred Thousand Songs of Milarepa, blessings are transmitted by teaching the nature of mind and reality through poetry and song. Although the ultimate nature of mind transcends description, poetry uses example to point to that which is beyond example. Just as a bird needs two wings to fly, so our experience is defined by the primordial intertwining of relative truth and ultimate truth, although we do not generally recognize this. Poetry is a means to unveil the ultimate within the relative.
—**Lama Norlha Rinpoche**, Meditation Master of the Kagyu Lineage of Tibetan Buddhism and Abbot of Kagyu Thubten Chöling Monastery/Retreat Center. He has also worked tirelessly to restore and preserve the cultural and religious heritage of his homeland of Tibet. He rebuilt Korche Monastery where he had received his training, founded a monastery and retreat center for nuns at the sacred site of Kala Rongo, and established schools and medical clinics in Nangchen, Tibet.

"Poets, like Buddhists, have trouble ignoring anything, even the smallest things. Lama Karma Chötso's alertness — quiet, tuneful, playful, true — to the world around her is the silent music of her poems. She takes us for a stroll in mindfulness, through an ever-renewing world."
—**Robert Kelly**, author of *Oedipus after Colonus*

# Dedication

This book is dedicated to
the Genuine Lamas of the
Kagyu Lineage of Tibetan Buddhism

and

Qing Hu

With special thanks to Angela Kelsey

In the time of the dragonfly
wings sparkle in humid air
and translucent bodies alight
on the leaves of the bodhi tree.

Immovable
between the tides
the river sings a quietude
no one can hear.

This is my home,
where every doubt has fled
and the power of uncertainty
lost its ground
as I found mine.

This is my home
because the earth speaks to me here,
tells me to settle this finite space
while orbiting the universe
beyond time
or life or death.

The talking rains of la selva
tell me stories
where past and future melt
one into the other
and the present
slips off a banana leaf
like a tear.

My dog barks a warning
inventing passing strangers again
or perceiving those
I can only imagine.

To rest for a time
beside the cascading water
I lean my back against a rock
        sun-warmed and solid and sleepy.
But the air whispers to my skin,
        "Stay awake!
        Stay awake!
        Every moment, wide awake!"

I'm trying to watch
what isn't there.
The masters say
it's impossible to see,
that my eyes are of no use
whatsoever.
If I'm careful
maybe I'll see it
with my ears.

Like a coven of strangers
we fly under the full moon.

As the light awakens
beneath our small plane
blankets of clouds
are painted in the pastels of sunrise.

“Is that you?
Are you really here?”
        he called across the room.
Stumped.
Who is here
to answer?

Fallen asleep with the ocean
outside the open window,
it's no surprise
that in the parody of dreams
I float and crash.

Awake late into darkness
as storms move overhead
pelting rain down
on the cottage roof.

Weary of lightning
and thunder
drumming its odd beats
over and over and over.

My only companion
is one little mouse
who's used to being awake
late into darkness.

No photograph
can capture consciousness,
freeze it,
then print it out
on an hp.

"Watch carefully,"
he said
as he walked
up the wall.

There's a certain airiness
to my body.
Where there should be bones
there is only a spaciousness
it would be sacrilege to fill
and impossible to place
in thought or motion.

My head is filled
with my mind.
So is my toe.
How could it be
otherwise?

If I could
I'd do it, too—
join you
in this escapade
of mourning.

It seems this wrenching
and tearing of the heart
will not subside
till I walk
stark naked
into the pain.

Before the morning fog scattered
I captured the day,
its entirety in one moment
already lived.

Today I danced
not because you died
four interminable days ago,
but because you lived.
Today I danced.

Just the touch of one finger
lightly on my shoulder
and I am the deity
in surprising fullness.

Fierce empowering consort!
In this embodiment of utter freedom
there is no need to fly.

I fed my fears to the fire.
Incinerated them.
They were hopeless,
without laughter,
and left no room
in a room
for breathing
or for love.

I fed my fears to the fire.
Torched them.
Burnt beyond recognition,
they cannot return
even as the charred remains
of guilty memory.

I have fed my fears
to the fire.

## Old Beginnings

Driving into past life territory,
kind fool behind the wheel
barrels down the highway
making time.

## The Wind

I'd like to talk to the wind.
I'd like to listen
as it tells me of its wanderings.
Then I would ask the wind,
"When you rest, do you die?
And when, careless and treacherous,
you carry us away,
do you feel our breath
become one?"

## The Apu

With every ray of sunlight gone
and the moon yet to rise,
the apus of the mountains come out,
filling the black air with their presence.

They brush against me from every direction,
with movements quick as thoughts,
sounds as soft as feathers.
Fanned by curiosity, they check me out,
me with my back hard against a tree.

## India

On the border
of this border town
I walk a dry, dusty road.
Ahead the shallow ditch
is filled with vultures
feeding on a horse carcass.
One of them turns,
rumbles toward me,
and enormous wings fly low
over my gasping head.

## Exhaustion

Achingly tired.
Crushed under the weight of
        attachment.
Finding no room
        inside this wheel
        of perpetual motion.
Notions of escape
escape in wisps of desire
        from the hellish depths
        of conceptualization.

## Night's Window

The tree frog's belly
presses against the glass
as he waits for the moths to fly
to the window's light.

Can he imagine
the stab of the heron's beak
in the morning?

## The Redness of Blood

Afternoon sunlight swirls over the bones,
stark white against darker sand.

A skull swings crookedly
on the arm of a black wooden cross
stuck in its eye socket.

The redness of blood
makes no appearance here,
where names a thousand years old
are not recalled by any living being.

Standing in this bardo between sand and sky,
lone holder of blood for a hundred kilometers,
I lean against the solid air
that breaks apart in desolation.

## The Condor

Black against the Andean sky
majestic winged sister
untethered in my dream
rides the thermals
of Colca Cañón.

## On Vacation

The world has slowed.
On the beach a man walks leisurely.
No one runs.
The seagulls move quietly over the sands
like small off-kilter ballerinas
choreographed without sound.
Even the sun sleeps in this morning
behind the grey clouds
of Chesapeake Bay.

## The Monastery

At the sounding of the gong
the trees applaud,
grasses ripple under the breeze,
and mind eases into place
like a rock coming gently to rest
after bouncing a long way
downhill.

## My Lama

To watch him walk
is to understand the path.

To try to keep up
is to miss the point.

## Lines for Cynthia

I thought I was following
        the light.
Then I thought,
        "The light is following me."
I decided to throw the light
as far away as possible,
        let it float free
        loose of its moorings
        straight into unimpeded endless space
        to illuminate it all.

## The Road

Met emptiness on the road today
who said, "You won't find me
by looking."

Turned then to the south
who said, "I have no end
and no beginning."

The center spoke not a word
of its absence
as I thought to settle there
in stillness
unidentified.

Learn to breathe,
    beating heart,
deeply
    and true.

In quiet rain
the tree drops its old leaves
to the water,
letting go
letting go

Sounds from a wind chime
drop gently on the breeze,
letting go
letting go

Mind illuminates the senses
and, naturally settled,
drops all thought expressions,
letting go
letting go

The old clock,
an afterthought
hung in the corner,
has found its own time zone.

The rhythm of the machine's motor
doesn't float on the melody
        of the spot-breasted oriole's song
nor synchronize with the sound
        of the woodland rains;
doesn't slow dance
        to the deepening beats
        of my pulsing heart
nor lift and soar
        with the achingly beautiful leap
        of the pink-bellied dolphin.

Holding
what cannot be held

the light of your essence

like the flash
of an unnamed star.

A child sings
words incomprehensible
high pitched
with no accompanying sense
though beauty of tone
and every mother
hears the hurtful call.

Caught
smack in the middle
of samsara.

Not one damned
enlightened leg
to stand on.

Blinded by age
with little left to remember,
he asks again and again
for a boat trip to the bay
where he used to catch
the best fish.

But always the son answers,
"Father, the sea is dead."

You've taken birth again.
In morning's dream
my hands themselves uncovered you,
pushed away the dark,
pulled you into me and,
knowing last I touched you was in death,
oh, how you were loved!

Not too far
from morning.

Stars still appear
in the ink of a pre-dawn sky.

Conscious of
tree branches scratching
against the window pane.

Conscious of
consciousness itself.

Beyond consciousness
no I
no tree
no more scratching.

Her lines of laundry
waving in the breeze,
she said,
“Thought I’d put
the wind to work.”

The barrier islands' curve
hooks the Atlantic waters
into its embrace,
forming an abstract design
unimagined by any artist.

Words flow like rivers,
carve deep canyons of meaning,
collect in iridescent pools
        of mirror-like reflections
before evaporating
        into their own empty air.

The desert that resides within
habituates the soul to arid climes
that open us to chance and change
beyond the mists that seek to hide
ourselves from ever brightening.

The goddesses flash
through the pacific airs,
move the outer forces and
inhabit the distances of space
alive within this corporeal form.

The ocean at low tide
reflects storm clouds on the horizon
and, silent as a mirror,
makes no comment.

Notes of peace
rhythm of compassion
wisdom's timbre
make a song of freedom.

So sing!
Sing the horizon
sing the streets
sing the unconditioned tones of love!

Is it words
that discern
the meaning
of words?

Who or what to mind
or take as true
in terms of minding
          you mind me now, girl
Can there be
a *you* minding a *me*
ultimately?
          you mind me now
          now, you, mind me
          habitually.

Though mind in now
is not now minding.

Fishermen drop their nets
into the bay,
then pull them heavy back to shore,
killing the small fish
caught by their tender gills.
The pelicans, the terns,
and the gulls
gather for a feast
while karma is generated
by the fistfuls
in one short morning.

The sounds of family
echo through millennia.
Countless echoes
of patience
more than love.

Interest in adding
to this world
diminishes
with the acceptance of,
inevitably,
leaving.

Rain falls on the river
water blending into water
as thoughts blend
into mind's
          hovering awareness.

The crystal beads
slide through her fingers,
effortlessly
counting mantras
while the deity resides.

Inside, mind shifts.

Outside, the dog lying on the floor
is myriad energies in movement.
The black cat is empty
of being a black cat.
And on the river the ducks,
the turtles, the fish
and the garbage
ride a flow of liquid light.

With the wisdom switch turned on
it's all divine illumination.

Look for the truth
in the silence
between the heartbeats
of the self.

Mind so easily expands
beyond its own concepts
in this selfless
vast sand and sky.

There is no difference
in stillness
and movement.

Nothing is still
and nothing moves.

What awaits, then, at the end?

All that is unfinished
still capturing the mind
in unending whorls
of manifestation?

What awaits is only
what is already here.

Discovering life
one breath at a time,
a small body stretches
new limbs.